Measures to Movements

Also by Diane Beth Garden
The Hannah and Papa Poems
Chapbook

Measures to Movements
Poems Inspired by Artworks

Diane Beth Garden

Negative Capability PRESS
MOBILE, ALABAMA

ISBN: 978-0-942544-75-6
Library of Congress Control Number: 2011941412

Published by:
Negative Capability Press
62 Ridgelawn Drive East
Mobile, Alabama 36608

www.negativecapabilitypress.org

Acknowledgments

I am grateful to Natalie Sandler, Jeff Goodman, Linda Burke, Anne Zelnicker, and the Canebrake Poets—Carol Case, Keri Coumanis, Vernon Fowlkes, Celia Lewis, and Sue Walker for their valuable suggestions.

These poems were originally published in the following journals:
Lagniappe - "Measures to Movements"
Mankato Review - "Schreiber Brothers"
Texas Center for Writers - "The Milkmaid"

TABLE OF CONTENTS

PREFACE

I love nothing more than standing and gazing at a painting in a museum. When my husband and I visit an exhibition, he is usually three or four rooms ahead of me. Sometimes, he will retrace and look for me, but not often. He knows as our daughter pointed out when a toddler, "painting is talking to mom." Something in the artwork catches my attention and holds me spellbound—the gold light that illumines and divides the space in *Philosopher Meditating* and *Stairway at Auvers*, the way the mothers bend over their daughters in *The Knitting Lesson* and *Blessed Art Thou among Women*, and the man's clenched fists in *Fortune and her Wheel*. In effect, a painting has chosen me, as opposed to my deciding to write about it before my visit to the museum. For this I am very grateful, for I realize this intense encounter between the painting and me will often lead to a new poem.

Of course, the painting poem does not write itself like "a found poem," one in which the words are taken from an outside text and left unchanged in the poem, except for elements of craft such as line breaks. Instead, I have to discover why the painting moves me—why I am excited, saddened, or disturbed, among many possible reactions. When I discover the core of my attraction, which is not always an easy task, I often realize that the painting is an "objective correlative," as conceived and defined by T.S. Eliot. A combination of aspects of the artwork correspond to an inner feeling or state of mind. While readers may not share my "experience," I hope they will see the painting from a new perspective and understand my state of mind.

The poems in this collection were written over the course of many years and grew out of my interest in art history (my minor in college), visits to cities with major museums, reading about artists' lives and studying reproductions of their paintings. While organizing my book, I discovered that a structure based on grouping poems with similar themes worked surprisingly well. These themes emerged, almost unbeknown to me, in contrast to choosing them in advance and writing poems that illustrated them. There are poems about intimacy (*Quiet Corners*), divisions and obstacles (*Barriers*), forms of love (*Desire*), resistance to obstacles (*Defiance*), and gratitude (*Blessings*).

I want to thank most of all the artists who struggled to create great works of art and to earn a living when they couldn't find buyers for their art. Their works invited me to enter the realm of contemplation and creativity.

Diane Beth Garden

For my husband Michael

Quiet Corners

The Milkmaid. Jan Vermeer. Oil, c.1658.

THE MILKMAID

For just a moment she has shed
all her troubles—the cow going dry,
her daughter's wheezing. She has let
it all fall away until nothing matters
but the cold and stubbly pitcher against
her hands, her basket filled with bread
and light. She knows her body fills
the narrow corner—that she can touch
a wall that is bare and cream-colored
and windowpane speckled brown like a bird,
that nothing matters, but the milk
falling in a braid to the russet bowl.

Snow at Giverny. Claude Monet. Oil, 1893.

4

SNOW AT GIVERNY

Monet knew we see more when we cannot see—
when snow makes the houses lose their shapes
and colors, we see beyond to purple shadows
delicate like lyric passages, beyond dark branches
to violet that hovers like perfume,
beyond names of bushes to their essence,
dark green swirls,
        and we hear the wind
by the slant of snowdrifts, and we know
snow is never white, but pearl and blue-grey,
forever changing like the sea, and colors
have weight from the way the roofs bend—
snow bonnets that hide the faces of houses.
While we cannot find doors or passageways,
we know we do not need them to enter.

Dancer Putting on her Shoe. Edgar Degas. Etching, c.1888.

DANCER PUTTING
ON HER SHOE

"To define is to destroy, to suggest is to create."
Stéphane Mallarmé

Degas did not dare offer the poet
Mallarmé his painting of a dancer
at the bench adjusting her slipper
with one leg behind her,
like a horse about to be shod.

He gave Mallarmé this dancer
who is drawn with simple lines
as in skywriting—a long line
for her leg, an arc for her back,
and swirls for her costume.

He knew Mallarmé's passion
for silence—he would admire
what is hidden in cream paper
more than any sign of a ballet
slipper with ribbons crisscrossing.

The Knitting Lesson. Jean-François Millet. Oil, 1852.

THE KNITTING LESSON

Her mother is tired and wants
to recede into the black background,
but she does not break her promise.
She joins her daughter in the dark
after housework and dinner.

The lamplight falls on their hands,
the beige ball of yarn, and basket
of blue shadows on her daughter's lap.
She cradles her daughter and waits
to see if her advice is needed.

She has already taught her to wrap
and purl without pulling too tightly,
to hide mistakes without unraveling,
and to make music clicking the triangle.
Soon, she will teach her how to cast off.

She does not realize her daughter
has learned more than how to knit.
She has shown her how to drop
her frustration and speak in a voice
as soft as her own golden shawl.

Boy with Spinning Top. Jean-Baptist-Siméon Chardin. Oil, 1783.

BOY WITH SPINNING TOP

He has finished his lessons
and pushed his books aside,
but he is not outside playing,
blowing bubbles or rolling a hoop.
He is standing at his table
with his back ruler-straight
like the bands on the wallpaper.
He looks like a miniature adult
with sausage curls and ponytail,
frock coat and stiff neckband.

Still, he is smiling as if someone
opened a window and a light
breeze graces his fine features.
Perhaps, he is dreaming his future—
the top turns into a boat with a tilted
mast that rocks on sea sheen,
and the pen and pincers in the drawer,
an octant for navigating by the stars.

Portrait of Estelle Musson De Gas. Edgar Degas. Oil, 1872-1873.

MEASURES TO MOVEMENTS

She has tucked herself into a corner
near the table where she is arranging
flowers she can barely see—
pale dabs and blurred bells in a vase,
a cloud of sea green and tan like the Gulf
when sand drifts up from the bottom.
She is mourning the steady loss
of her vision—flowers whose bright
rose, white and vermilion have faded.

Soon, she will be prepared to live
with total blindness among shadows.
She is learning to draw the world closer
as her fingers bathed in white light bless
the flowers, the way she will grace keys
as she plays first measures then movements.

Grainstacks, End of Day, Autumn. Claude Monet. Oil, c. 1890-1891.

GRAINSTACKS, END OF DAY, AUTUMN

When a farmer bundles
and stores hay in the barn,
he brings on winter, miles
of brown yellow stubble,
like a playground deserted
after daylight with swings
and seesaws at a standstill.
Monet preferred this field
with grainstacks in clusters
that looks like a village
of thatched cottages, turning
rust and gold at sunset.
People are savoring the last light—
a father sits near the window
with his daughter on his lap
who giddy-ups with glee.
A couple lingers under eaves.

Barriers

Bathers. Paul Cézanne. Oil, 1890.

BATHERS

The bathers are stopped in time—
as if playing a children's game of freeze,
one with a towel in a loop on his arm
like a lasso, another with his hand
in the air, one lunging about to dive.
These naked men, enclosed in a circle,
are idealized with bodies molded
after the principle of golden proportion.
It is as if Cézanne painted a sign:
Women are forbidden to enter.

Philosopher Meditating. Rembrandt van Rijn. Oil, 1632.

THE SPIRAL STAIRCASE

He spent the day
on one side of the spiral staircase
that winds from floor to ceiling,
with gold window light falling
on the passage from *Exodus*
he probed and pondered.
Now, he is nodding and drifting,
tired from turning and lifting words
in late afternoon that became
as heavy as mud bricks.
He is dreaming he untangled
the text and is sharing at shul.

He has forgotten
his wife who spent the day,
standing at a table at the market
selling potatoes, onions, and eggs.
He does not hear her worries hissing
as she bends over the kindling.
How will we manage tomorrow
if so many eggs are spoiled?
He does not know she wants
to learn Hebrew and dreams
she holds an iron above her head—
to smash the stairs that divide them.

Stairway at Auvers. Vincent Van Gogh. Oil, 1890.

THE GOLDEN STAIRS

Even though the old women in navy and green
    are on the winding path, and they are poised
    as if to spring,
everything is against them reaching the top
    of the golden stairs.
They could never get past the green man
    who looks like a night watchman.
The stairs are rocking like a suspension
    bridge, and the banister is slippery.
And those steps—some are toppling over
    like dominoes, and others are too steep,
    rising like a cliff without footholds.
They are already tired from taking in laundry,
    frocks and crinolines worn by young girls
    like the ones behind them.
Even if they make it to the top, no one will open
    the windows or doors painted shut.
If only they would walk around the corner, past
    the shed with yellow shafts shooting from the roof
    like sparklers,
they might find something unexpected, something
    better than golden stairs.

Sick Mother and her Children. Käthe Kollwitz. Lithograph, 1920.

24

SICK MOTHER
AND HER CHILDREN

The daughters gather at the foot
of their mother's bed in a room
with a fragment of a table,
white space for a blanket,
and grey walls with ragged edges.

The mother's face is crisscrossed
with worry over her family.
She is too weak to beg the grocer,
and her neighbors can no longer
spare any scraps of food.

The daughters, thin like wafers,
wear dresses that are pencilled in,
smudged from erasing in the wash.
The elder sisters bow their heads,
helpless without money for a doctor.

The little one looks straight ahead.
She does not understand why
her mother can barely speak,
why her sister holds her back
and keeps her far from her mother.

Blessed Art Thou among Women. Gertrude Käsebier. Photograph, 1899.

MINISTERING

Look, she does not notice
your hand on her shoulder,
the way you are leaning over,
lingering as if you want
to prevent her from leaving.

I can see all the preparation—
you cut her bangs and brushed
her hair. You soothed her
when she told you Molly
made fun of her during class.

Soon, you will have to step back
to let her go off to school.
You will need to stay busy.
First, put away the china, plate
after plate, saucer into saucer.

You must not become disappointed
if she comes home crying.
Even with all that ministering,
you cannot stop Molly from pulling
away your daughter's friend at recess.

Portrait of a Creole Planter. Jacques Guillaume Lucien Amans. Oil, c. 1835-1845.

PORTRAIT OF A CREOLE PLANTER

When I look at your shirt
with all those pleats
like an accordion half open,
I see an ironing board,
a sad iron, and a slave wiping
her brow with her bandana.
When I look at your buttons
those shimmering opals,
I see bolls of cotton,
and think of the hours
a slave bent over
to pay for one of them.
When I look at your hands
soft and plump
that show no sinews,
I see her hands cracked
and ripped from picking,
blued from lye in the laundry.
When I look at your lips
sensuous and smug,
they tighten and turn cruel.

Desire

Circle of the Lustful. William Blake. Illustration of Dante's *Inferno*, Canto V. Watercolor, 1826-1827.

32

The Circle of the Lustful

Dante does not forgive those who sinned
through flesh that blinded them to reason,
the lusty who fornicated with kin,

and spouses whose desire led to liaisons
that betrayed their marriage vows,
sexuality that spiraled into treason.

Dante condemns them like sows
in a pen or slaves packed in a ship
with cells too small to stand or bow

to a whirlwind that winds whip,
blue green coils that are narrow
like intestines where shades stripped

of dignity, flesh without marrow,
twist their necks and fling their arms
and howl as they are tossed in furor.

Yet, Blake leaves a pair out of the swarm
and places them in a circle of blue white light.
Paolo and Francesca are not harmed

for reading about Lancelot the knight
his love for Guinevere, the kiss
that inspired and led to their own plight.

Woman Combing her Hair. Edgar Degas. Oil, c.1887-1890.

CELLO SOLO

Degas opens the curtain that falls
in folds of blue, violet and gold
and invites us into her chamber
to listen to her body's music—
her flushed pink arms, breasts
that rise and taper to nipples,
and russet hair laced with blue light
that flows between her breasts
onto her robe pooled on her lap.

Petunia. Georgia O'Keeffe. Oil, 1925.

36

PETUNIA

This flower in a white stone jar
against curtains with blue grey
in the ridges looks like a woman
who is waiting for her lover.
When he arrives, she will not turn
off the lights, or hide under
the sheet, but will guide his hand
to her sweet violet folds and invite
him to enter her dark chamber.

Defiance

Fisherman's Mother. Helen Mabel Trevor. Oil, c.1893.

FISHERMAN'S MOTHER

She sits on a stoop bearing witness
to sorrow like a war widow
who places a cross on a hilltop
in honor of her husband.
She wears her grief in heavy layers,
a blue cloak over her jacket
and a hood that hides her hair.

She remembers that night
when she could not sleep with wind
whipping and shutters flapping.
She set up her stand at the market
in the dark and waited for light,
for her son with his bucket of fish.
The men never found his boat or body.

Still, she looks forward and smiles,
a beacon for others who are lost.
Mornings she lifts the blue beads
and silver crosses on her walking stick
to pray and contemplate the Mysteries.

Fortune and her Wheel. Jack Yeats. Pencil and Poster Paint, 1902.

FORTUNE

The men afraid of their futures
need to end their uncertainty.
They leave hearths for heavy coats
and wait under winter skies, anxious
to pay the gnome for their turn.

They have forgotten the last man,
who shook when the wheel stopped,
spat at Fortune and staggered from the ring
where he stands with clenched hands,
fist in his mouth, with no one to fight.

The Oarsmen (The Schreiber Brothers). Thomas Eakins. Oil, 1874.

THE SCHREIBER BROTHERS

The wake of gold bathes the brothers'
arms and faces, turning their sticky shirts
to silk and pain to perseverance. The coach
hidden in the deep brown background
waves frantically his megaphone.
Blades buried in the mahogany river
push the water and defy resistance.
Light kindles their red bandanas
like the sun behind stained glass that dyes
Mary's faded robe royal blue. It cascades
over the side of the boat, leaving gold
lines that zigzag across the river. I want
to hold this moment like a crystal bell
about to ring. I never want to plumb
the dark parts to find broken eggshells,
to hear how they fought over lunch.

Woman with a Parasol, Facing Left. Claude Monet. Oil, 1886.

Woman with a Parasol, Facing Left

Monet could not stop the neighbors
from gossiping about him and his Alice,
but he could with only his palette
and his wooden box of brushes
paint her daughter in a long white
dress that falls in flutes, holding
a parasol filled with sea green light,
and wearing a veil of lavender sky.
In this meadow of wild flowers,
nothing is more disturbing than wind
that flares and flings her scarf.

Landscape with Cows, Sailing Boat and Figures. August Macke. Oil, 1914.

FACES WITHOUT FEATURES

We cannot tell what is near or faraway—
a sailboat tacks on a lake above trees.
Orange and rust cows glow like charcoal.
A circus barker tips his hat and floats
sideways in the sky, defeating gravity.
Only faces without features
foreshadow the Great War, the battle
where Macke lost his life and magic.
If only we could push the colored panes,
we might enter a new dimension.

Artist's House Seen from Rose Garden. Claude Monet. Oil, 1922-1924, Inventory 5086.

Artist's House Seen from Rose Garden. Claude Monet. Oil, 1922-1924, Inventory 5087.

RED THEN BLUE

"He feared the dark more than death."
Artistsguilds Directory

When his eyes failed him
and could not filter colors,
Monet painted from memory,
imagining his palette with white,
rose, and purple that he once
turned into parasols, water lilies
and snow on cathedral stones.
He missed colors the way
he longed to hold Camille in bed,
a scent he could only dream.
He could no longer see details—
the double railing on the Japanese
bridge became a green flurry.
Still, he continued painting
until he died, even when the house
in the rose garden turned red
then blue, as he closed an eye.

Blessings

Abraham and the Three Angels. Marc Chagall. Etching, 1956.

THE ANNUNCIATION

Three angels
with wings
as dazzling
as sun on snow,
appeared
in our garden.

They promised us
in spring
we would have
a child.
We bowed
in the grass.

I made ready
to serve them,
spreading the table
with an embroidered cloth,
with honey cake
and wine.

While they picnicked
with their wings
open like butterflies,
you stood
under a tree
beaming.

55

Houston Street. George Luks. Oil, 1917.

HOUSTON STREET

The vendors wave and cry out
to direct the traffic to their carts—
Pickles 1 Cent, Bananas 4, Eggs 3
The women rush—splashes of red
and yellow—to buy what they still
need for Sabbath, more celery
and carrots for soup on the stove.

Two girls in blue and white
stroll apart from the crowd, free
for now of mothers and chores.
But soon prices will fall, mothers
will call, and streets will empty
as crowds funnel into tenements
to finish preparing for Sabbath.

Before sunset families will gather
at tables set with best dishes,
challah and wine glasses.
Mothers will kindle candles,
circle their hands over light,
cover their eyes and chant blessings
to welcome in the Sabbath.

Still Life with Onions. Paul Cézanne. Oil, c. 1885.

STILL LIFE WITH ONIONS

When we look at these onions, we cannot
imagine a housewife at a market in Provence
holding one in her hand and turning it
as she searches for dark places.
Cézanne removed the onions from the earth
by brushing them with celestial colors—
pink, white, and rose, and placing
them on an altar cloth with a chalice,
against a mauve and blue background
that carries us beyond the kitchen table.

LIST OF ILLUSTRATIONS / CREDITS

Quiet Corners

Page 2: Jan Vermeer, *The Milkmaid*, Collection Rijksmuseum, Amsterdam

Page 4: Claude Monet, *Snow at Giverny*, New Orleans Museum of Art: Loan from the Mrs. Frederick M. Stafford Collection. EL.1977.9

Page 6: Edgar Degas, *Dancer Putting on her Shoe*, c.1888, Art Institute of Chicago, The Joseph Brooks Fair Collection, Photography © The Art Institute of Chicago

Page 8: Jean-François Millet, *The Knitting Lesson*, St. Louis Art Museum, 106:1939

Page 10: Jean-Baptist-Siméon Chardin, *Boy with a Spinning Top*, Louvre, Paris, Courtesy of Art Resource, N.Y.

Page 12: Edgar Degas, *Portrait of Estelle Musson De Gas*, New Orleans Museum of Art: Museum Purchase through Public Subscription. 65.1

Page 14: Claude Monet, *Grainstacks, End of Day, Autumn*, 1890/1891, Oil on canvas, Coburn Memorial Collection, 1933.444, Art Institute of Chicago, Photography © The Art Institute of Chicago

Barriers

Page 18: Paul Cézanne, *Bathers*, c.1890-1892, Musée d'Orsay, Paris, Courtesy of Art Resource, N.Y.

Page 20: Rembrandt van Rijn, *Meditating Philosopher*, 1632, Louvre, Paris, Courtesy of Art Resource, N.Y.

Page 22: Vincent van Gogh, *Stairway at Auvers*, St. Louis Art Museum, 106:1935

Page 24: Käthe Kollwitz, *Sick Mother and her Children*, Käthe-Kollwitz-Museum, Berlin, © 2010 Artists Rights Society, N.Y.

Page 26: Gertrude Käsebier, *Blessed Art Thou among Women*, © Metropolitan Museum of Art, N.Y.C, Courtesy of Art Resource

Page 28: Jacques Guillaume Lucien Amans, *Portrait of a Creole Planter*, New Orleans Museum of Art: Gift of Mr. Emile N. Kuntz. 78.209

Desire

Page 32: William Blake, *Circle of the Lustful*, © Birmingham Museum & Art Gallery, Birmingham, England

Page 34: Edgar Degas, *Woman Combing her Hair*, c.1880-1882, Musée d'Orsay, Paris, Courtesy of Art Resource, N.Y.

Page 36: Georgia O'Keeffe, *Petunia*, 1925, San Francisco Museum of Modern Art, Bequest of Elise S. Haas, © Georgia O'Keeffe Museum, Courtesy of Artists Rights Society, N.Y.C.

Defiance

Page 40: Helen Mabel Trevor, (1831-1900), *Fisherman's Mother*, Photograph Courtesy of the National Gallery of Ireland

Page 42: Jack Yeats, *Fortune and her Wheel*, 1902, Pencil and poster paint on card, Courtesy of the Niland Collection, The Model, Sligo, Ireland

Page 44: Thomas Eakins, *The Oarsmen (The Schreiber Brothers)*, 1982. 111.1, John Hay Whitney Collection, Yale University Gallery, New Haven, Ct.

Page 46: Claude Monet, *Woman with a Parasol, Facing Left*, 1886, Musée d'Orsay, Paris, Courtesy of Art Resource, N.Y.

Page 48: August Macke, *Landscape with Cows, Sailing Boat and Figures*, St. Louis Art Museum, 911:1983

Page 50: Claude Monet, *Artist's House Seen from Rose Garden*, Musée Marmottan, Inventory 5086 and 5087.

Blessings

Page 54: Marc Chagall, *Abraham and the Three Angels*, in honor of Ebria Feinblatt (M.84.192.8) Los Angeles County Museum of Art, Courtesy of Art Resource, N.Y., © 2010 Artists Rights Society

Page 56: George Luks, *Houston Street*, St. Louis Art Museum, 121:1972

Page 58: Paul Cézanne, *Still Life with Onions*, c. 1885, Musée d'Orsay, Paris, Courtesy of Art Resource, N.Y.